ABC Reading eggs

Level 1
Activity Book s

MW01046024

1 Join the **n** things to Nutty newt.

2 Hop over to the **nuts**.

Nutty newt

3 Draw 9 nuts in the nest.

Nine nuts

4 Trace.

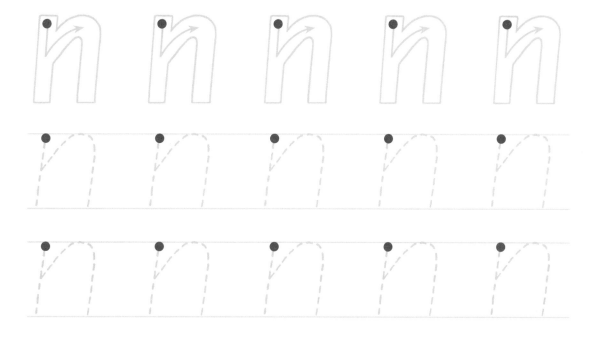

Lesson 12

PpPpPpPp

1 Join the **p** things to Pinkipoo.

2 Hop over to the **p** food.

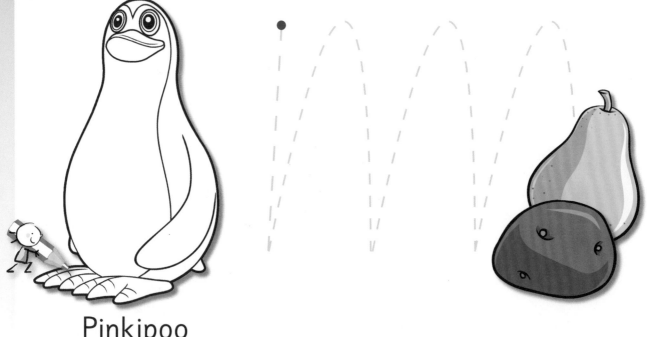

Pinkipoo

4

3 Draw some pepperoni on top of the pizza.

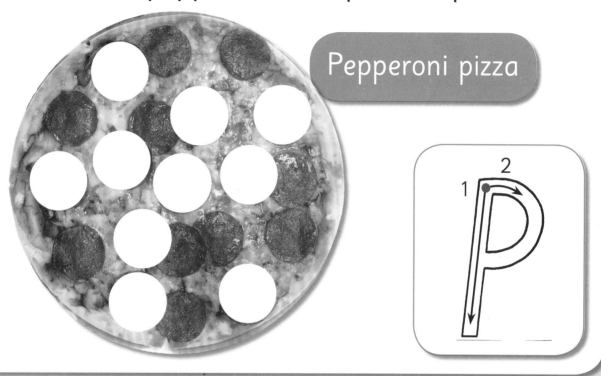

Pepperoni pizza

4 Trace.

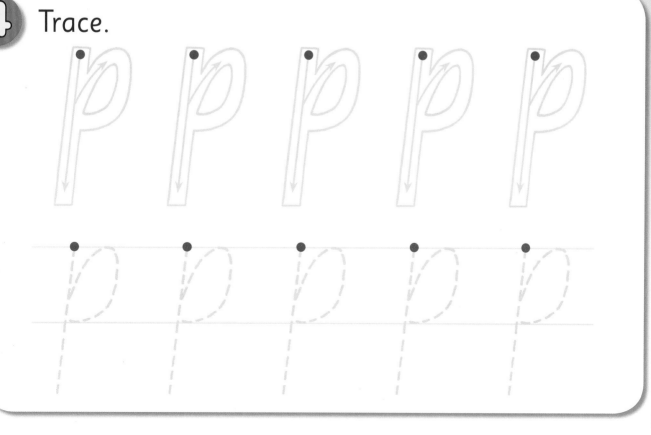

1 Match each word to a picture.

ant

bee

cap

fish

nut

tap

map

sun

2 Read each sentence. Join it to a picture.

I am Sam.

Sam pats a cat.

Sam pats a bat.

Sam pats a fat cat.

7

Fun spot 1

1 Complete the dot-to-dots.

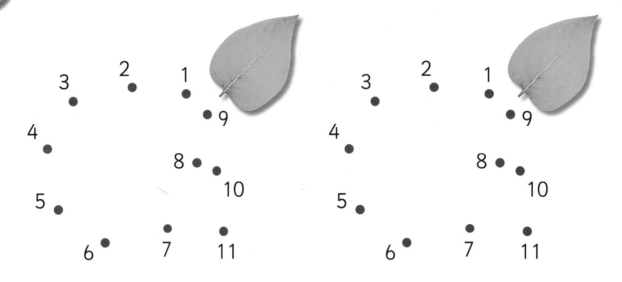

2 ✏️ all the **N**.

J	N	H	M	L	Y	N	E
A	N	N	V	S	U	N	F
Z	N	D	N	X	W	N	I
Y	N	L	R	N	Z	N	J
X	N	B	O	D	N	N	O
R	N	A	P	U	C	N	A

3 Jump across the lily pads. I yellow, **am** red and **Sam** blue.

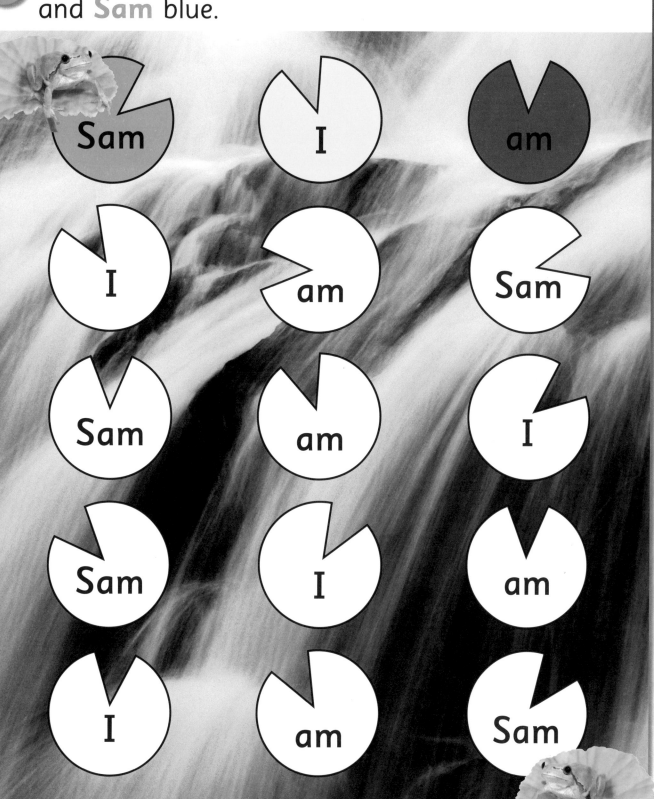

1 Join the **h** things to Horse hee heepo.

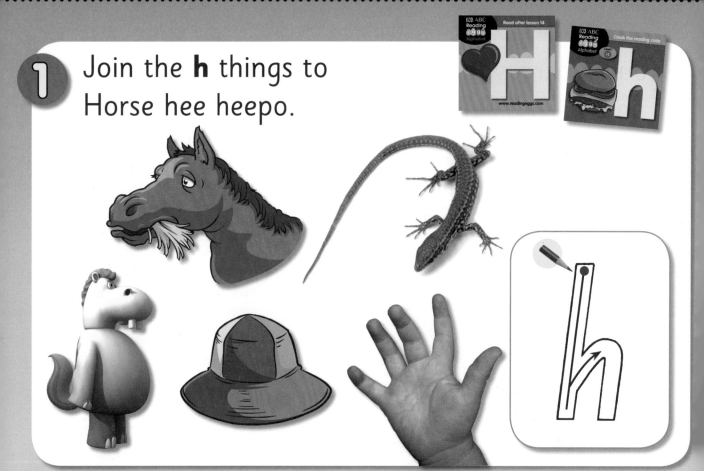

2 Drop the ball into the hole.

Horse hee heepo

3 Draw a house on a hill.

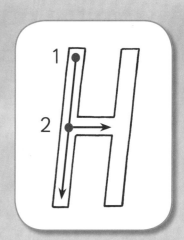

House on a hill

4 Trace.

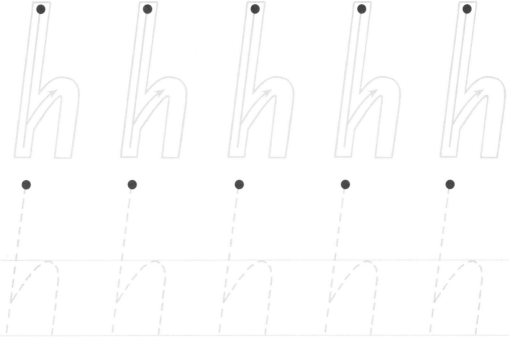

Lesson 15

RrRrRrRrRr

1 Join the **r** things to Red rabbit.

2 Run over to the **r** food.

Red rabbit

3 Give each robot a recorder.

Robots with recorders

R

4 Trace.

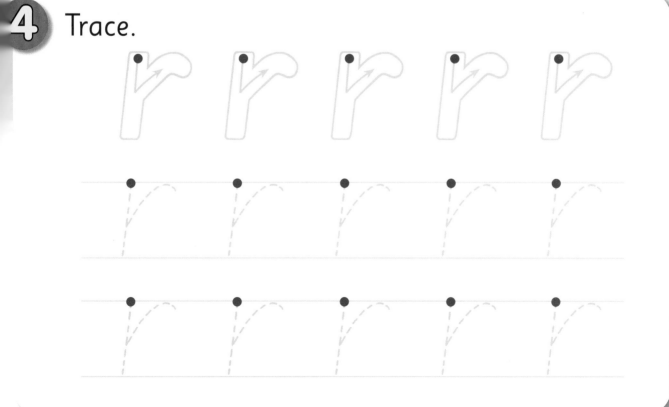

1 Join each critter to their food.

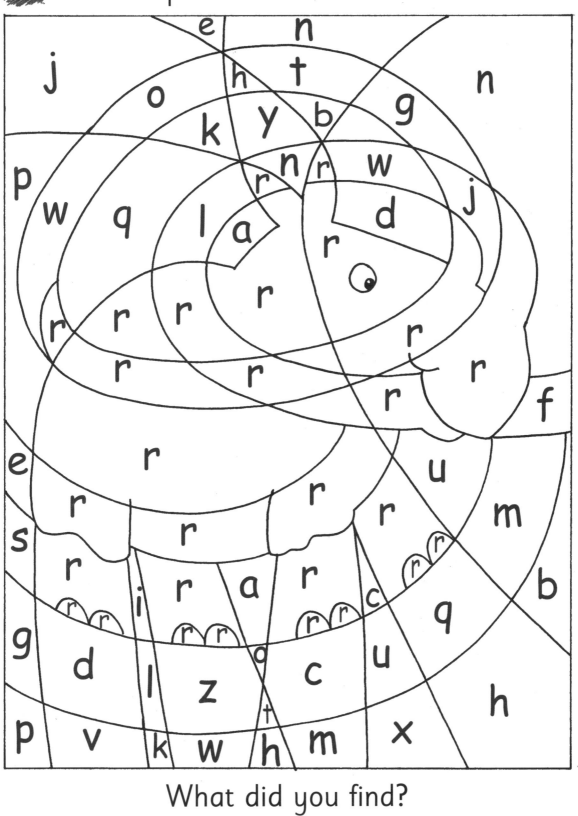

2 all the **r** parts.

What did you find?

1 Complete each sentence.

Sam can

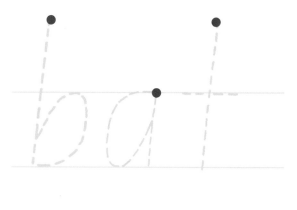

A man can

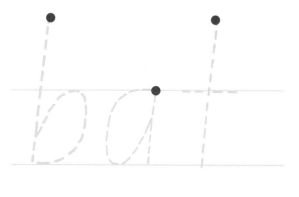

man
cat
rat

2 Finish the sentence with one of these words. Read each sentence.

I am a

_____

I am a

_____

I am a

_____

1 Join the **z** things to Zebstar.

2 Draw some zigzags.

Zebstar

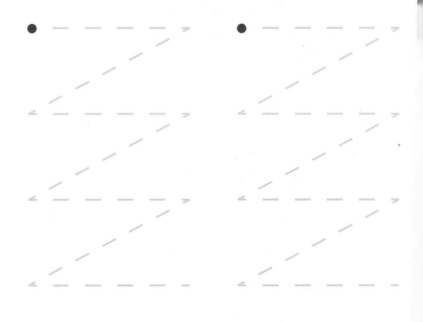

3 Draw some **zzz** on the sleeping zoo.

A zoo going to zzz

4 Trace.

1 Join the **e** things to Eggyphant.

2 Join the word to the picture.

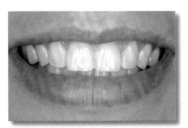

bee

tree

see

teeth

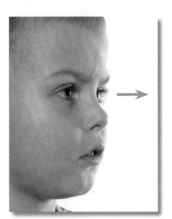

ABC Reading eggs

3 Eggyphant's egg.

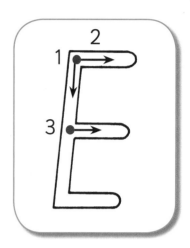

Eggyphant is an eggy elephant.

4 Trace.

Fun spot 3

1 Circle pictures that start with the letter.

n

p

h

r

2 Join the rhyming words. Words that rhyme sound the same at the end.

rat

can

fan

mat

man

cat

bat

sat

tan

ran

Lesson 19

hat
cat
pan
man

1 Write the matching word.
Use one of these.

2 Choose the right ending for the sentence.
Cross out the wrong one. Read each sentence.

Sam can see

the man.

the pan.

Sam can see

the bat.

the hat.

1 Add an **s** when there is more than one.

1 cat

2 cats

1 bee

2 bees

2 Choose the right ending for the sentence.
Cross out the wrong one. Read each sentence.

Can you see

the 3 bats?

the 4 bees?

Can you see

the 5 cats?

the 5 bees?

Fun spot 4

1 Join each thing to the right letter.

h

z

r

28

2 Follow the paths for each word.

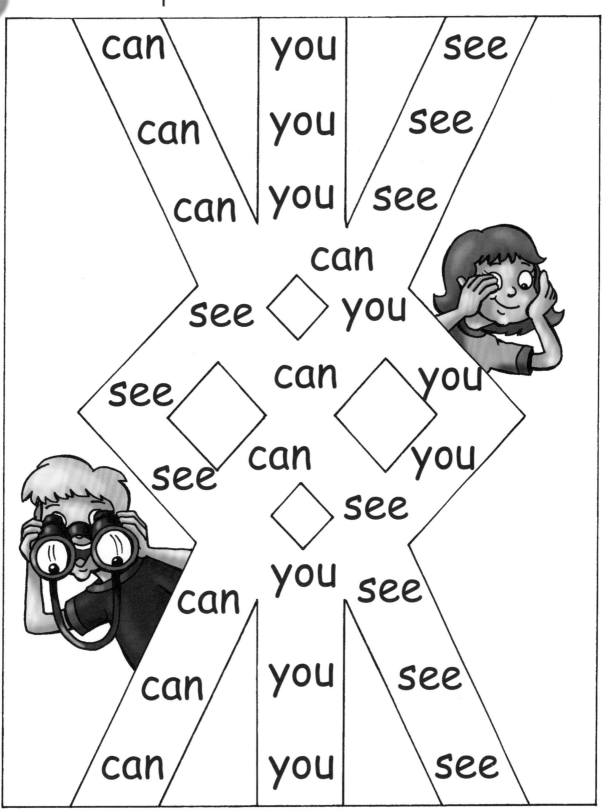

can you see
can you see
can you see
can
see can you
see can you
see can you
can
see
you see
can you see
can you see

1 Trace and ✏.

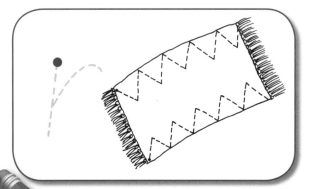

2 ✏ the letters you know.

a	b	c	d	e	f	g	h	i
j	k	l	m	n	o	p	q	r
s	t	u	v	w	x	y	z	⭐

3 Match to a picture.

hat

pan

rat

man

bees

Sam can see.

WOW!
Now you are reading!